D0762166

44169480

ART FROM

ROCKS AND SHELLS

with projects using pebbles, feathers, flotsam and jetsam

Gillian Chapman & Pam Robson

Wayland

SALVAGED!

Art from Fabric
Art from Packaging
Art from Paper
Art from Rocks and Shells
Art from Sand and Earth
Art from Wood

This book was prepared for Wayland (Publishers) Ltd
by Globe Education, Nantwich, Cheshire

Artwork and design by Gillian Chapman
Photography by Rupert Horrox

First published in 1995 by
Wayland (Publishers) Ltd
61 Western Road, Hove
East Sussex BN3 1JD

Printed and bound by
G. Canale & C. S. p. A., Turin

British Library Cataloguing in Publication Data

Chapman, Gillian
Art from Rocks and Shells. - (Salvaged Series)
I. Title II. Robson, Pam III.
Series 745.5

ISBN 0 7502 1529 1

Acknowledgments
Special thanks to Richard Grogan, Isle of Wight C.C. Nature Reserves
Warden, for his help in identifying and supplying feathers used in the
projects, and Martin Simpson, The Fossil Man, Blackgang Chine, Isle of
Wight for supplying the fossils and minerals used on pp. 6-7.
Photographs on p. 4 bl Tony Stone/David Young Wolff and on
p. 5 br Werner Forman Archive/Manitoba Museum of Man & Nature.

Contents

Weathered Treasures   4

Rocks and Fossils   6

Pebbles and Stones   8

Making Mosaics   10

Shells   12

Board Games   14

Feathers   16

Weaving Materials   18

Rope and Shell Masks   20

Moving Collages   22

Flotsam Notice Boards   24

Green Messages   26

Tide Time   28

Glossary   30

More Information   31

Index   32

Weathered Treasures

Rocks

Rocks can be found anywhere. The type of rocks that you find will depend upon the area in which you live. Look at old buildings built from rock. Observe signs of weathering – rock can be shattered by frost action, it can also be dissolved and discoloured by acid rain. Statues and headstones in graveyards are often carved from rock. Many gravestones are granite, a hard-wearing igneous rock. Others are marble, a metamorphic rock. You can observe which headstones have weathered most quickly by examining the lettering carved there – is it still legible?

Shells

Shells are only found by the sea but different shells are found on beaches in different parts of the world. The nature of a seashore is decided by the type of rock found there. Some seashores are sandy, others may be rocky, shingle or even mud flats.

Rubbish Pollution

We frequently read true horror stories about seashore creatures killed by oil pollution at sea. Many coastal areas are polluted by sewage discharged into the water. Rivers too are often polluted by industrial waste. Avoid such areas when searching for recyclable treasures. On the shore, shells, waterweeds and pebbles lie scattered amongst the flotsam and jetsam that drifts ashore from passing ships. Each time a wave crashes on to the shore another exciting collection of bits and pieces is strewn at random, just waiting to be found.

Beachcombers roam the seashore in search of such treasures. Always take care when collecting – there may be broken glass or other dangerous items.

Young beachcombers examining their find.

Collecting Rocks and Shells

Inland waters wear away the rocks, often carrying fragments for many kilometres. Look near rivers, ponds and lakes for interesting rocks but always take care when near water, especially deep water. The best places to find rocks are cliffs and quarries but both can be dangerous places for children. Never visit either without an adult.

To find rocks, shells and pebbles try looking in caves or beneath cliffs, in rock pools and between the tide marks.

Weather and Tides

Most of the world's rivers eventually flow into the sea. Rivers carry debris from storms and weathered fragments of rock. Once these waters enter the salty sea they are carried away by the tides and currents. Where the materials are found will depend to a great extent upon the weather and the tides. A particularly stormy day or an exceptionally high tide can bring some unusual finds. When you search will also make a difference. If you are writing a project, keep a record of your discoveries. Write down the time of day and the date, as well as the weather conditions.

Preparation

Before you set out to collect your treasures, gather together the necessary equipment. Have a notebook and pencil for recording details, and take plastic bags in which to carry your finds. Dress in suitable clothing and footwear.

Caution

Be careful by deep water and fast flowing rivers. When searching by the sea always check tide times, as the seashore can be a dangerous place if the tide is coming in. Always replace shells containing living creatures. Wash all found items in fresh water when you return home, before doing any of the projects in this book.

Stone men near Hudson Bay in Canada were built by the Inuit to help them catch caribou.

5

Rocks and Fossils

Collecting Rocks

Rocks can be rough or smooth in texture. They vary in colour from light to dark, and may be heavy or light, but most will be angular in shape. Loose pieces of rock are broken from rock strata as a result of weathering or erosion.

Never climb dangerous cliffs in search of rocks. You will find an amazing variety beneath the cliffs and on the seashore. When you have gathered an interesting assortment arrange them in order of colour and texture.

Recognizing Rocks

Rocks are composed of minerals. Some contain a mixture of minerals, others, such as chalk, are single mineral rocks. Granite is a very hard rock. It contains many minerals, one of which is quartz, a crystalline substance found in many forms. Quartz can be a gemstone, flint or sand.

You can identify the rocks in your collection by referring to information books or visiting a geological museum with your drawings and notes.

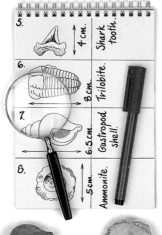

Keep drawings and notes of the rocks and fossils that you collect.

To make the corners of the display box, cut flaps, fold over and glue.

Plan for Making a Display Box for Rocks and Fossils

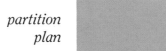

partition plan

◄ *partition marks*

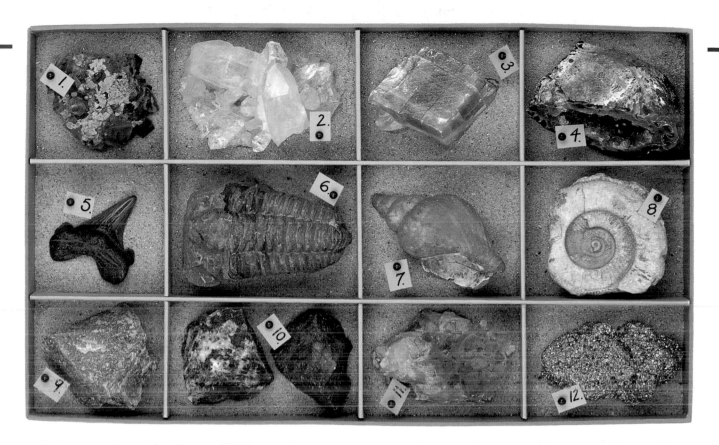

Rock and Fossil Collection in a Display Box

Add labels with a key to tell people about your collection.

Fossils

The natural history of our Earth can be seen in rocks. Marine or sedimentary rocks often contain fossils of ancient plants and sea creatures, like ammonites. The ammonite is related to the nautilus, a sea creature living today, that existed when dinosaurs roamed the Earth.

Cataloguing the Collection

Information about rocks and fossils can be obtained from expert sources so you can classify your collection accurately. Keep a detailed record of each item in a notebook. Label your specimens and give each an individual code or number. Then cross-reference the rocks and fossils with the written information.

Making a Display Box

Choose the most interesting specimens from your collection for display. To make a box large enough to contain them, first arrange the rocks and stones on a piece of paper. See how much space each piece needs and plan out the position of the partitions.

Cut out the box shape from a piece of thick card. Fold and glue the sides together. Make the partitions from strips of card the same height as the box. Cut slits in the partitions where they cross and slot them together. Put a layer of sand or sawdust in the bottom of the box as a cushion for your collection. Label all the partitions so each rock can be identified.

Pebbles and Stones

Pebbles

Pebbles of all sizes are found by water. They are always, by their very nature, smooth in texture, but they may be flat or rounded in shape. The shape of a pebble depends upon the kind of rock from which it has been weathered.

Attrition

A pebble can be as small as a marble or as large as an egg. Its smooth shape is caused by a weathering process known as attrition. This happens when rocks are rubbed continuously against each other. Rounded pebbles are formed from hard rocks because they are worn evenly all round. Flat pebbles are weathered from rocks containing many different layers or strata. The layers show as bands of colour in the pebbles. Pebbles are hard, they can be heavy or light.

Pebbles formed from different rocks.

Pebble Patterns

Cobblestones

A cobblestone is a large, naturally rounded stone. On the east coast of England there are cottages built of cobblestones. These are not the same cobbles used to build roads.

Colour, Shape and Texture

When you have made a collection of pebbles, wash them and group them together according to colour, size and shape. Try arranging your collection into simple patterns. Many artists gain inspiration for their work by observing the natural world around them.

Men of Stone

Giant stones formations, like Stonehenge in south-west Britain, were constructed thousands of years ago. In some places, as on Easter Island in the Pacific, their original purpose remains a mystery. They may have been used as calendars marking the sun's path through the year. In the Boothia area of northern Canada, rows of giant stone men can be seen. When a small group of hunters tracked caribou, these men of stone frightened the herd in the direction of the hunters.

Stone Man

Pebble Faces

Pebble People

Collect together stones and pebbles of different colours and size. Make simple stone figures and faces by balancing pebbles on top of each other. These arrangements need only be temporary, but if you want your work to last, glue the stones together with PVA adhesive. A thin coat of PVA painted over the models will dry as a clear varnish, bringing out the natural colours of the stone.

Making Mosaics

Mosaics in History

Pebbles have been used as the raw materials for mosaics for centuries. The earliest pebble mosaics had a practical purpose as floor coverings. The Romans used pieces of marble to create elaborate pictures on walls and floors. These mosaics can still be seen today.

Archaeologists have uncovered Roman mosaics in many parts of the world. Recently, in northern Israel, a mosaic centaur was uncovered for the first time in the floor of a building. It is thought to be 1,700 years old. It was found at the site of the ancient city of Sepphoris, the capital of Galilee in Roman times.

Group pebbles together by colour.

Arrange the pebbles on scrap paper referring to your design.

Aztec Mosaics

Later in history, the Aztecs used mosaics to create masks from small squares of semi-precious stones like turquoise. One example has been found on which they were laid over an actual skull; even the original teeth are still there.

Collecting Materials

Pebbles and shells are ideal for mosaic making. You will find them in every colour and shape. Smooth pieces of coloured glass also look attractive in a mosaic picture. Collect as much material as you can before taking it home to clean.

Sketch out a design for your mosaic on squared paper keeping it very simple – it is surprising how much material you will need to complete a small pattern.

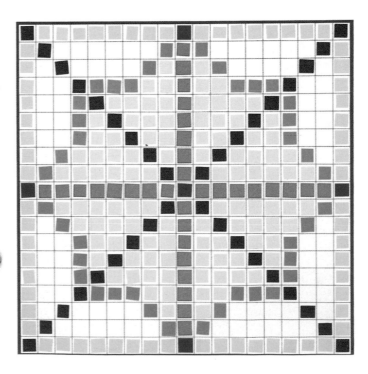

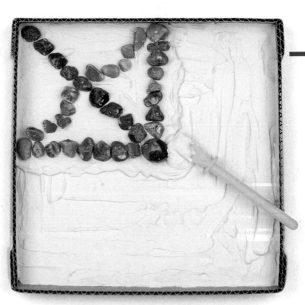

Making a Mosaic

Mosaics are a permanent form of pattern-making. Once you have planned and worked out a design, the pieces are embedded into a plaster base. First sort your materials into piles according to colour, shape and size. Then lay out your mosaic on a piece of scrap paper, following your design. At this stage you can move and rearrange the pieces until you are happy with the effect.

Making a Plaster Base

From your design, work out how large your finished mosaic will be. Then make a cardboard mould the same size and about 5 cm deep. Mix up some plaster following the instructions on the packet, and pour it into the mould to a depth of about 2 cm.

Transfer the design on to the plaster base.

Transferring the Mosaic

Wait until the base is hard before transferring the mosaic pieces. Coat a small area of the base with a thin layer of fresh plaster. Stick the mosaic pieces into the fresh plaster keeping to your design. Work quickly before the plaster sets. Continue across the base until the mosaic is complete.

Pebble Mosaic

Shell Medallion

11

Shells

Molluscs

Empty shells are found along most seashores. They once belonged to molluscs – creatures with soft bodies and no inner skeletons. Gastropods are univalves with a single coiled shell, like a periwinkle. Look carefully to see whether a univalve coils in a clockwise or an anticlockwise direction. Bivalves are molluscs with two shells held together by a muscle. The two halves of a mussel shell are the same size but this is not the case for all shellfish.

Collect together a variety of shells. Look at the different colours, patterns and shapes – are any of them symmetrical? Are they shiny or matt, translucent or opaque? They will all be very fragile.

Shells through History

Shells were once used as currency in some parts of the world. The Indians of the north-west coast of America traded with long strings of tusk shells. The Aztecs used huge conch shells as trumpets during their religious ceremonies. In ancient Jericho, when someone of importance died, the face was fitted with a death mask and cowrie shells were placed over the eyes to make them look life-like.

Shell Jewellery

Necklaces, bracelets and hairbands can easily be made by threading shells on to thread, ribbon or elastic. First arrange the shells in order of colour and size. Look for shells that have naturally occurring holes, ready for threading. Otherwise, ask an adult to drill holes in the shells for you.

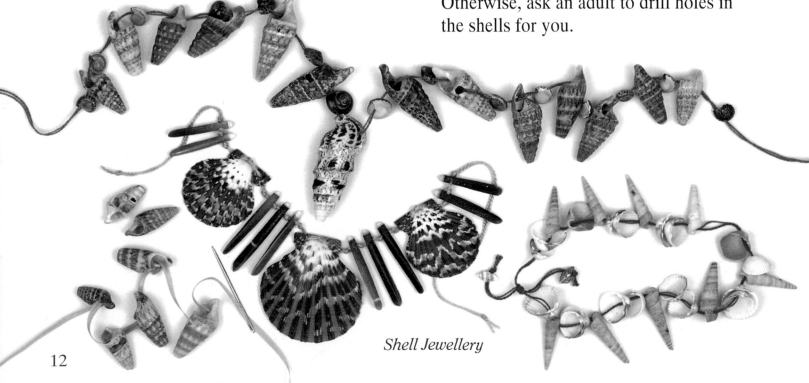

Shell Jewellery

Shell Mobile

Mobiles

Making mobiles and windchimes from shells is an ideal way to use and display your collection. A mobile needs to be a balanced arrangement. Suspend the shells from a branch. Choose attractive shells of different sizes and hang them on varying lengths of thread. Arrange the shells so the mobile is well balanced, possibly using the heaviest shell at one end and counter-balancing it with several smaller shells.

Windchimes

When making a windchime, you should choose the lightest shells so they will move gently in the slightest breeze. Tie strings of shells to a supporting branch. The lightest wind will cause them to chime as they move and touch.

Hang your mobiles and chimes outdoors in a special place that you have found in a garden or by water. Leave them there to move in the breeze, making music for others to enjoy.

Shell Chimes

13

Board Games

Ancient Games

Natural materials like pebbles, bones and shells have been used for centuries to make accessories for games. The first calculator, known as an abacus, was probably pebbles arranged in grooves of sand. The Ancient Egyptians enjoyed board games. Squares were marked on a huge block of stone to create a senet board.

The game of mancala has been popular for centuries across Africa and Asia. Boards were made out of wood and seeds were used as counters. The Aztecs played a game called patolli which was like backgammon. Each player had pebble counters. You can do what the Ancient Egyptians did and use a flat stone to make a board game. This game is called tic-tac-toe, or noughts and crosses.

Pebble Abacus

Tic-Tac-Toe

Find a large flat stone to act as a board and mark it out with nine spaces, as shown here. Collect two sets of smaller stone counters, of different colours. The player who first makes a line of three counters wins.

Tic-Tac-Toe Stone Board and Counters

Shell Game

You will need some large deep shells such as scallop shells, to act as catching trays, plus some smaller shells or light pebbles to throw. Place the large shells with the inside uppermost and mark each with a score. From an agreed distance throw the small pebbles one at a time into the large shells. Players should have an equal number of throws. The highest score wins.

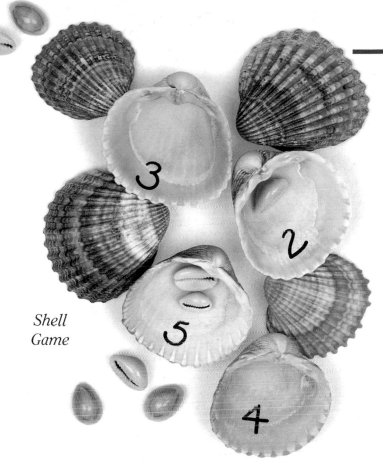

Shell Game

Laying Out Kai-Awase Shells

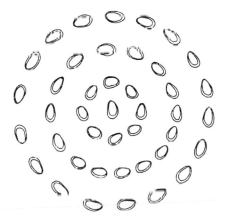

Painted Shells

A shell game, called kai-awase, was first played in Japan centuries ago, using beautifully decorated bivalve shells. To make a similar shell game, first find 20 pairs of bivalve shells, such as mussels or cockles. Paint a matching pattern or design on each half of the shell. These are mixed up with all the other decorated pairs and arranged face downwards, as shown here. Players take it in turns to turn two shells over. If they pick a matching pair they keep them and have another turn. The player with the most pairs wins.

Painted Shells

15

Feathers

Collecting Feathers

From time to time, birds of all sizes and colours shed their feathers. You may find feathers when you are out collecting rocks and shells. Feathers are light, but very strong. Numerous barbs project from each side of the central shaft and each barb in turn bears smaller interlocking barbules with tiny hooks.

Try and identify the feathers by looking in reference books. Record your findings in a feather book. Make slots in the pages and thread the feathers through. Sketch the birds from which the feathers have come and make notes about how they nest and feed and where they choose to live.

Seabirds

Feathers found on the seashore will be those of seabirds like gulls, gannets and guillemots. The guillemot nests on rocky cliff ledges and lays eggs that are narrow at one end. This prevents the eggs from rolling off the ledges.

Pollution

Oil spillages and the disposal of industrial waste can cause great harm to the flora and fauna of rivers and seashore alike. Look out for signs of pollution. Birds are the first to die when oil covers the water. Oil soaks into their feathers and stops them from working properly. The birds cannot keep warm and die from cold.

Feather Book

Herring Gull
Habitat : sea cliffs, dunes, lakes and reservoirs.
Nests on cliff ledges, laying 2-3 eggs.
Adult bird - 56-66 cm.

Black Headed Gull
Habitat : very commonly found inland as well as coastal areas, marshes and estuaries.
Very social bird - a roost may consist of 10,000 birds.
Adult bird - 36 cm.

Aztec Featherworkers

The Aztecs were superb craftspeople, skilled in the craft of featherwork, using a technique passed down from generation to generation. They would use the feathers of exotic birds like parrots, or dye the feathers of less colourful birds. A beautiful design was worked on a background of specially prepared cotton.

Aztec Fan Decorated with Shells

Feather Sculpture

You could use your collection of feathers to make a 3-D sculpture. Feathers are light and easy to glue or tie together. Depending on the overall shape of the sculpture, bundles of feathers can be bound together. Single feathers can be stuck into a base of self-hardening clay, or glued onto card. Decorate the finished sculpture with small pebbles and shells, and paint if necessary.

Aztec Fan

First make a circular card base, with a stick handle. Glue layers of feathers to the base, overlapping the feathers and decorating the centre of the fan with small shells. If you are using white and grey feathers you can colour the fan with splashes of paint.

Sculpture made from Feathers, Shells and Driftwood

Weaving Materials

Rushes and grasses

As you collect materials alongside lakes, rivers and estuaries, you will also find tall straight rushes that are perfect for weaving. Plants that grow by the sea must protect themselves against salt spray and strong winds. Observe the leaves and roots to see how they differ from inshore plants. Even their shape is different.

Marram grass has very long roots. It is planted on sand dunes to prevent them from being blown away. In dry weather, marram grass leaves roll up into narrow tubes to trap damp air inside. Near the high tide mark you will find sea lyme grass, where dry sand has blown from the shore. Above the high tide mark, sea couch grass grows. Marram grass grows throughout sand dune areas.

Gathering Materials

Before you set out to collect materials, check first with an adult that they can be freely picked. If too much marram grass is removed, sand dunes can be blown away. As weaving materials, most grasses are ideal as they have long flexible stems. Try weaving other branches and stems into baskets, especially if they have interesting colours and textures.

Storing and Using Materials

Weaving materials can be hung in a cool, dry place until required, but they will dry out and may need to be soaked before they can be woven. If they are freshly picked they should still be supple. To test the materials, wind a small piece around your wrist – if it snaps it is too dry and needs soaking.

Starting a Base

First cut eight pieces of thick grass, each about 40 cm long. These grasses are called the stakes. Lay them in a cross shape as shown here. Choose a long length of grass, called the weaver, and weave it around the cross several times to make the basket base.

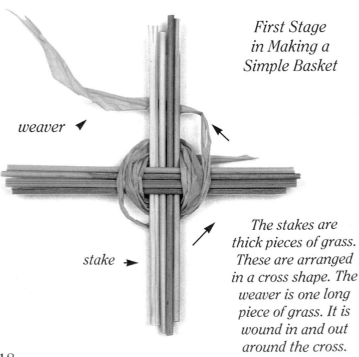

First Stage in Making a Simple Basket

weaver

stake

The stakes are thick pieces of grass. These are arranged in a cross shape. The weaver is one long piece of grass. It is wound in and out around the cross.

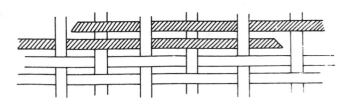

Adding a New Weaver

Weaving the Basket

Continue weaving the weaver in and out of the cross, as shown here, separating the stakes and weaving in and out of them. You may need to add extra weavers as you work. Just lay the new weaver next to the old and carry on weaving them together.

To make your basket attractive, weave in grasses with their seed heads still attached. Carry on weaving until the basket is large enough, but make sure you still have 15 cm of the stakes left free for finishing off.

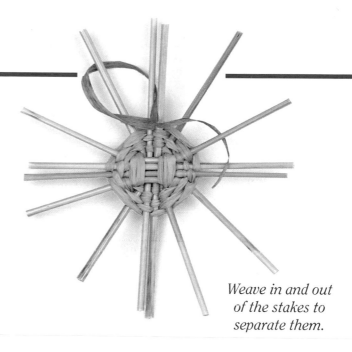

Weave in and out of the stakes to separate them.

Finishing off the Edge of the Basket

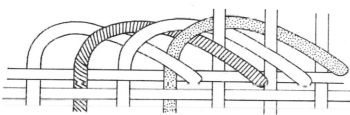

Finishing off

To make a neat border along the top of the basket, bend each stake over as shown here and tuck in the ends. You may need to soak the stakes first before you continue. Decorate the finished basket by attaching shells and small pebbles with strong thread.

Baskets Decorated with Shells

19

Rope and Shell Masks

Traditional Masks

Look in museums and books at examples of artefacts made hundreds of years ago by the ancient tribes of Africa and South America. You will find fascinating masks made from all types of fibres and natural materials, intricately decorated with shells, feathers and precious stones.

The Iroquois Indians of North America made masks of corn husks to wear during ceremonial dances. In New Guinea, the tradition of making basketry masks continues today. These masks are woven from fibres and cane, and are covered with cowrie and nassa shells.

Mask Template

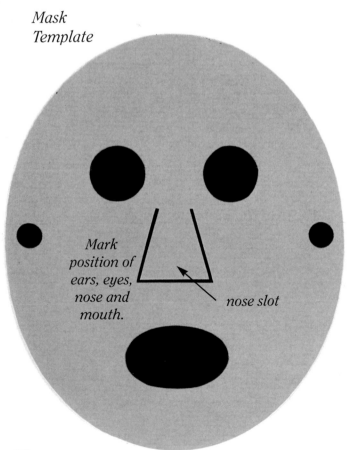

Mark position of ears, eyes, nose and mouth.

nose slot

Flotsam and Jetsam

Amongst the exciting finds that you will come across at the water's edge will be lengths of rope and netting, carried by the current from passing boats. It is always a good idea to pick up items of this kind because they can endanger wildlife. Found objects like these can also be put to many good uses.

Making a Rope and Shell Mask

First you will need to collect together quantities of rope and string. Try and salvage as many different types as you can – rope comes in many colours and thicknesses. The more textures you use the more interesting the design will be. Also collect together shells, feathers and pebbles to decorate the finished mask.

Making a Mask Template

Cut out an oval shape from a piece of thin card, making it slightly larger than your face. Hold it up in front of your face and ask a friend to mark on the card the positions of your eyes, mouth, ears and nose. Cut out holes for eyes and mouth. Make a slot around the nose shape as shown here. The ear marks also indicate the position of the holding string needed to tie the mask around your face.

Decorating the Mask

Cover the card template with PVA glue and arrange lengths of rope and string over the shape. Use the string to make the facial features. Coil it around the eye holes and mouth, being careful not to cover over the holes with string. Fray the rope to make hair and use different coloured strings to highlight the various features. Add shells and small pebbles to complete the face. Try to cover up the whole card template with textures.

Leave the mask to dry. Pierce two small holes by the ear marks. Thread through a length of string to attach the mask to the head.

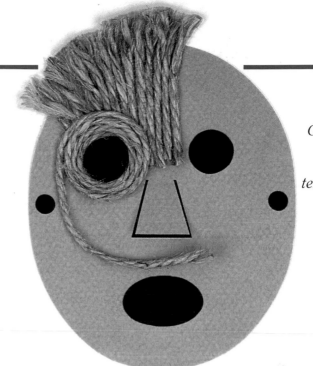

Glue the string to the template.

Shell Mask

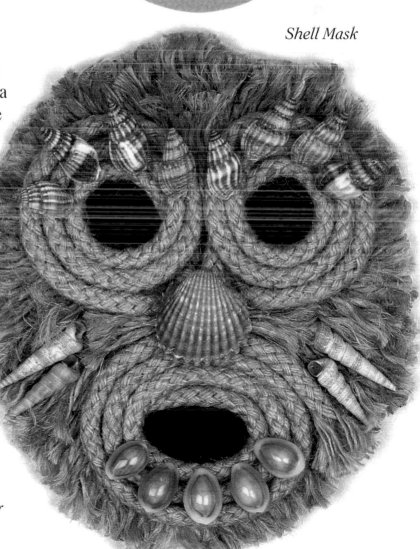

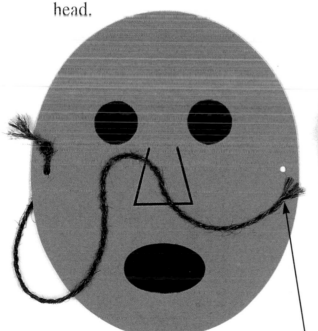

Back of Mask

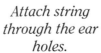

Attach string through the ear holes.

21

Moving Collages

Movement on the Shore
The shore is a scene of constant change. Weather, currents and tides combine to move and carry flotsam and jetsam, shells and seaweed – all manner of exciting things – to and fro. Each day you will find something new.

Movement at Sea
Out at sea, ships and boats move backwards and forwards, battling against, tides and currents, gales and breezes. By using a mixture of natural materials and flotsam and jetsam, you can create some unusual moving collages. Collect and sort your materials first. Do they suggest a subject for a picture, possibly an underwater scene?

Designing the Collage
First sketch out your design on scrap paper. Think about which parts of the collage could move. In an underwater scene, fish could be made to swim along. You will need to mark the lines along which the fish will move, as shown in the sketch below.

Preparation
Find a piece of strong card which is large enough to take your design. You may like to paint the card with a background scene first. Trace the design on to the card making sure you mark the lines of movement clearly. These will need to be cut into slots before you start glueing the rest of the collage to the card.

Collage Material

Sketch for Moving Collage

Finished Collage

Thread moving parts and sticks through the slots and move them from side to side.

Assembling the Collage Picture

When you have sorted and cleaned all your collage materials – shells, pebbles, dried water weed, sand – you can begin to construct the picture. Take care to keep the movement slots clear. To make the moving parts, cut out shapes from card and decorate them. Glue each shape to a long stick, then thread the sticks into the picture. The moving parts can be moved from side to side, along the slots, controlled from below.

Making the Fish

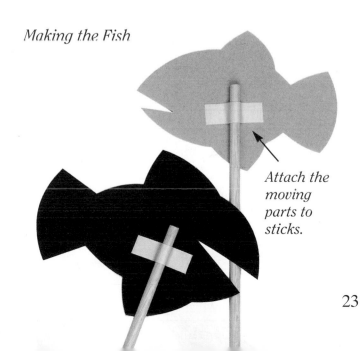

Attach the moving parts to sticks.

23

Flotsam Notice Boards

Purposeful Projects

By recycling flotsam and jetsam found on the shore – driftwood, pebbles, shells, rope – to use in purposeful projects, you are helping conserve Earth's resources. To design and build useful artefacts out of found materials is the best kind of recycling.

A notice board is a practical, useful object. Using left-over cork tiles, or thick cards, as a base you can create a unique driftwood frame, decorated with shells and pebbles. This is a perfect way to display a holiday postcard collection.

Constructing the Board

Decide upon the size of the finished board, bearing in mind that the framework will take about 10-15 cm all round. Cut out the basic board shape from thick cardboard.

You may need to glue several layers of corrugated cardboard together for added strength. You want your board to be strong and durable. If you have cork tiles use them to cover the top surface, making sure they are stuck fast with strong glue.

Constructing the Board

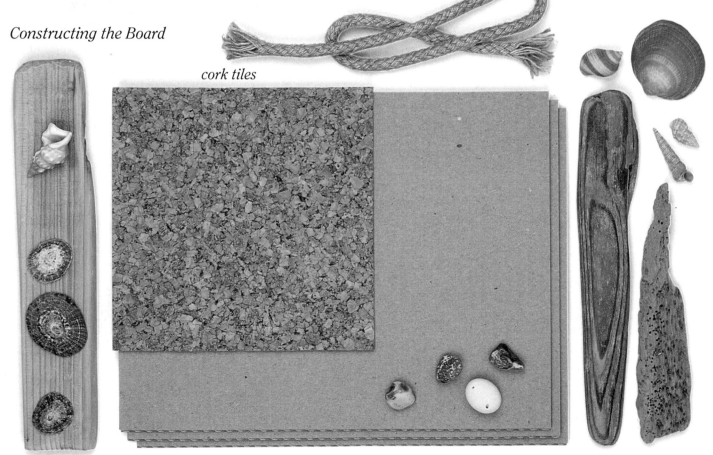

cork tiles

frame pieces

Glue several layers of card together.

Making the Frame

Sort out the materials you intend to use for the frame. Allow plenty of time for damp materials, like the rope and driftwood to dry out before using. Position the materials before glueing anything down permanently. Put large pieces of driftwood and coils of rope around the edges first. Smaller items like pebbles and shells can be arranged on top of these. When you are pleased with the final arrangement glue everything in place with a strong glue.

Rope Notice Board

Driftwood Notice Board

Green Messages

Our Environment

Our shores and river banks should be a world full of treasures waiting to be enjoyed and appreciated, but all too often they have the appearance of rubbish dumps. We are polluting our planet, and our waterways and seashores often reflect the appalling damage that is being done. Litter is strewn at random, oil smothers wildlife and destroys habitats, sewage and industrial waste pour into the water. What can you do to help?

Green Messages Collage

Use items like sand, shells and feathers and black paint for tar.

Litter Patrol

Organize a regular litter patrol. When you walk along a river or seashore take with you a rubbish collection bag. Pick up any litter, but beware of broken glass or other dangerous objects. If in doubt ask a grown-up. You will probably find metal cans or glass bottles that can be placed in recycling bins.

Green Messages

Use some of the cleaner rubbish to make a collage or 3-D sculpture that conveys a strong message to others, such as a warning against pollution caused by rubbish dumped in seas and rivers.

Green Poems

If you enjoy poetry you will have found many poems that talk about the environment. Have you read one that expresses your feelings exactly? If so, try illustrating it with a collage of found objects and natural materials. Write out the poem and mount it with your ideas on a backing of stiff card.

Green Tree Poem

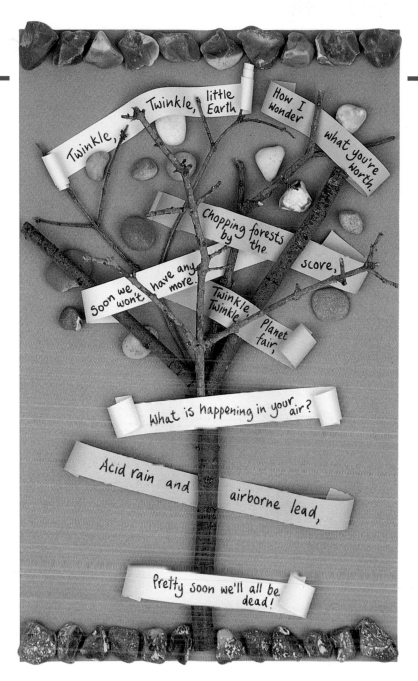

Twinkle, *Twinkle, little Earth* *How I wonder* *What you're worth.*

Chopping forests by the *score,*

Soon we won't have any more.

Twinkle, Twinkle Planet fair,

What is happening in your air?

Acid rain and airborne lead,

Pretty soon we'll all be dead!

Make the tree from a piece of twig and decorate with pebbles.

Messages on Bottles

I was walking on the beach when I saw a pool

The waves were plastic bottles And the pebbles were bottle tops....

Then I remembered a pool where the pebbles were solid gold...

And rainbow fish darted in crystal water.

Write your own poems on labels you have fastened to plastic bottles.

Message on a Bottle

You may enjoy writing your own poems. Can you write a poem that will show how strongly you feel about the environment? If you find a clean empty plastic bottle on the shore or floating in the water, you could attach your poem to the outside and display it. Others will then read your message.

27

Tide Time

Tides and Timing

In some parts of the world, the tide comes in and goes out twice a day. Tides occur because of the gravitational pull between the moon, the Earth and the sun. The highest point on the shore, reached by the tide, is called the high water mark; the lowest, the low water mark.

Roughly once a fortnight there are spring tides, which are nothing to do with the season of spring. They rise higher and fall lower than neap tides that occur between each spring tide. A naturalist can recognize zones on the seashore in which certain plants and animals of the shore prefer to live. Land-locked seas, like the Mediterranean, have very little tide movement. Lakes have hardly any at all.

Pebble Sundial

The first means of checking the passage of time was by observing the shadows made as the sun passed overhead. This was only possible on sunny days, out-of-doors.

On a sunny day a sundial can be made by the water's edge. Collect together some large pebbles to mark the hours and a stick to use as a pointer. The position of the shadow cast by the pointer marks the movement of the sun and the passing of the hours. Refer to a watch to position the pebbles or shells accurately at hourly intervals. Smaller pebbles could mark the parts of the hour. Take your pebble sundial home and reassemble it in the garden.

Pebble Sundial

Shadow Clock

A shadow clock could be made in a similar way to the pebble sundial, using materials found on the beach. Find a piece of flat driftwood to act as a base and fix a stick at one end, upright and at right angles to the base. When the sun shines this will cast a shadow. Throughout the day as the hours pass make a mark in the base to record them, or use shells as markers. A shadow clock records the position and the length of the shadow during the day.

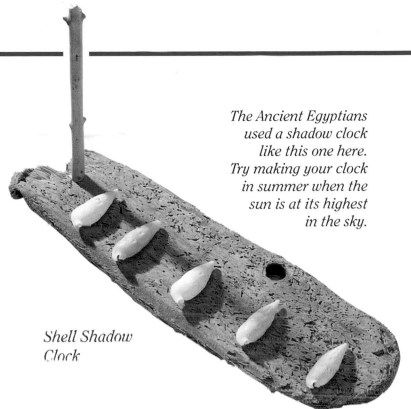

The Ancient Egyptians used a shadow clock like this one here. Try making your clock in summer when the sun is at its highest in the sky.

Shell Shadow Clock

Driftwood Clock

Driftwood Clock

A simple structure resembling a real clock can be made from natural materials and flotsam and jetsam found on a beach or beside a river. Collect together materials – pebbles, shells and pieces of driftwood. You will need to take them home to construct the clock.

Choose a flat surface for the clock face and two sticks for the hands. If you want the clock hands to rotate you will need to get an adult to help you drill holes in the centre of the face and in each hand. These can be fixed in place on the clock with a nail. Use shells or pebbles to mark the hours and decorate the completed clock with natural materials. This clock may not tell the time but you will enjoy passing the time looking at it.

29

Glossary

abacus A simple tool used for counting. Each stone (or bead in a modern abacus) represents a number.

acid rain Rainfall made acidic by air pollution from cars and power stations. It damages forests, rivers, lakes and buildings.

attrition The wearing away of rocks as they rub against each other, usually in water.

barbs The hairs that make up a feather. Tiny interlocking hairs are called barbules.

beachcombers People who search the seashore for objects of interest or value.

bivalves Mollusc shells that are made up of two hinged parts.

centaur A creature from Greek mythology which had the head, arms and upper body of a man and the lower body and legs of a horse.

currency This usually refers to money. Money is commonly exchanged for goods.

debris Fragments left when something is broken.

erosion/weathering The wearing away of rocks by natural elements such as water.

estuary The place where rivers enter the sea.

flora and fauna The plant and animal life found in a particular area.

flotsam and jetsam Traditionally, flotsam was floating wreckage. Jetsam, shortened from jettison, described materials thrown overboard from boats to lighten the cargo. The phrase now means items 'littering the shore'.

habitat The natural home of a living thing.

igneous Rocks that have formed from magma and lava that has hardened, usually deep underground.

metamorphic Rocks that gradually change over time due to pressure and heat from the inside of the Earth.

minerals Natural substances like diamonds, that are usually mined from the ground. Rocks are made of minerals.

molluscs Soft-bodied animals that usually have a shell, but no backbone.

sedimentary Rocks made up of layers of weathered igneous rock, usually formed beneath the sea and often containing fossils.

shingle The coarse gravel and pebbles on a seashore.

strata Layers of sedimentary rocks.

univalves Mollusc shells that are made up of only one part. (See also bivalves).

More Information

Books to Read

Allen and Brown, *The Last Green Book on Earth?* Red Fox, 1994

Carlson, L. *EcoArt,* Williamson Publishing, 1993

Davidson, R. *What is Art?* Oxford, 1993

Oliver, R. *Rocks and Fossils,* Hamlyn, 1993

Petrash, C. *Earthwise,* Floris Books, 1993

Temple, L. *Dear World,* Bodley Head, 1994

Terzian, A. *The Kids' Multicultural Art Book,* Williamson Publishing, 1993

Woolf, F. *Picture this Century,* Hodder & Stoughton, 1993

Written by Children of the World, *Rescue Mission Planet Earth – A Children's Edition of Agenda 21*, Kingfisher, 1994

Addresses for Information

Australia

Australian Conservation Foundation, 340 Gore St, Fitzroy VIC 3095

Canada

Canadian Museum of Nature, PO Box 3443, Station D, Ottawa K1P 6P4

UK

Friends of the Earth, 26-8 Underwood Street London, N1 7JU

London Ecology Centre, 45 Shelton Street Covent Garden, London, WC2 9HJ

Marine Conservatory Society, 4 Gloucester Road, Ross-on-Wye, Herefordshire, HR9 5BU

Royal Society for the Protection of Birds, The Lodge, Sandy, Bedfordshire, SG19 2DL

Rock Watch, The Green, Witham Park, Waterside South, Lincoln, LN5 7JR

Rescue Mission Headquarters, Peace Child International Centre, The White House, Buntingford, England, SG9 9AH

Places to Visit (UK)

Natural History Museum, Cromwell Road, London, SW7

Museum of Mankind, Burlington Gardens, London, W1X 2EX

Geography
1. Geology/fossils /minerals and mining/ rocks and plate tectonics /volcanoes
2. Weathering/erosion
3. River systems
4. Sand dunes/desertification
5. Weather and climate
6. Acid rain/air pollution.
Local study – a litter survey

Language and Literature
1. Onomatopeia/ alliteration/water/ seashore sounds
2. Green poems
3. Posters carrying environmental messages
4. Research skills
5. Folklore/ legends of shipwrecks and pirates
6. Treasure

Art and Craft
1. Making tools
2. Collage
3. Patterns
4. Moving parts
5. Making jewellery
6. Masks
7. Weaving
8. Mobiles

Topic Web Art from Rocks and Shells

Design and Technology
1. A gravestone survey Properties of materials
2. Joining materials
3. Combining materials
4. Strengthening materials
5. Balanced structures
6. Mounting and displaying collections

Science
1. Sun and Moon
2. Tides and time
3. Gravity
4. Shadows
5. Sundials/shadow clocks
6. Making observations
7. Keeping records
8. Ecosystems/habitats
9. Pollution/the environment
10. Natural history – birds and flight
11. Living things – classification – invertebrates/ vertebrates/ molluscs

History
1. Famous shipwrecks — The *Mary Rose*, the Armada, the *Titanic*
2. Smugglers and pirates
3. Francis Drake
4. Ancient History — the Romans, Ancient Egypt

Maths
1. Symmetry
2. Patterns in nature/ spirals/the nautilus
3. Coiled shells/ direction
4. Board games